RESPONSIBLE PARENTING AS A MEANS OF AVOIDING THE

ARMAGEDDON OF 2054

WALTER S. FOSTER

Barringer Publishing, Naples, Florida
www.barringerpublishing.com
Cover, graphics, layout design by Lisa Camp

ISBN: 978-0-9908209-2-5

Library of Congress Cataloging-in-Publication Data
Responsible Parenting as a means of
Avoiding the Armageddon of 2054
Walter S. Foster

Printed in U.S.A.

This is a work of fiction. All characters, organizations,
and events portrayed in this novel are either products of the
author's imagination or are used fictitiously.

DEDICATION

To:
Elizabeth B. Foster
My patient and loving wife

TABLE OF CONTENTS

PREFACE

NEWSFLASH: NASA announced today that Asteroid 1728 will crash into the Atlantic Ocean seventy-five miles northeast of Bermuda on December 28, 2054 at 10:14 am EST. At the point of impact, Asteroid 1728 will weigh 107,054 tons and create waves in excess of 200 feet. Asteroid 1728 will destroy all cities within twenty miles of the East Coast of the U.S. as well as the Western Coast of Europe. NASA added that they have no means currently available of altering the course of the Asteroid or lessening its impact.

The President of the United States said he had today appointed a special commission to investigate steps to be taken to alter the course of Asteroid 1728 and that he would be meeting tomorrow with the G20 to coordinate global efforts. A Gallop poll showed that 98% of the public approved the President's response and were counting on the government to alter the course of Asteroid 1728.

Because the threat of the impact of a huge asteroid is a precise "hard" logical knowledge (i.e. a threat to our physical life),we would expect the President of the United States to react immediately to try to prevent this threat.

On the other hand, we know today of disasters of equal magnitude based on approximate "soft" emotional threats to life that we are quite content to ignore. For example:

> **HUMAN INTEREST:** The United Nations announced today that the world's current population of 7.3 billion will increase by 33% by December 2054 to 9.8 billion. Developing nations will account for 95% of that 2.5 billion increase.

> The Press Secretary for the President of the United States said that the President had not seen the article but would have no comment. A Gallop poll showed that 98% of the public had not seen the article. The remaining 2% of the respondents felt that the article was important but that there was little that we could do about the situation.

A population increase of 2.5 billion will have as dramatic a negative impact on our lives as an asteroid like Asteroid 1728. Because the effect of a 33% increase in of the world's population is "soft" emotional conceptual knowledge (i.e. a threat to the quality of life rather than a threat to physical life), we act as if we can do nothing about it.

As a result, we end up with war, aids, divorce, genocide, and economic depression as the only means to correct human ignorance and inaction about long-term psychological catastrophes. The question is why do we feel a threat to our psychological life is less important than a threat to our biological life?

The answer would appear to be that evolution has programmed us to listen to our external physical threats before listening to our internal sensual satisfaction. It would appear evolution has programmed us to listen to our external logical knowledge before we listen to our internal emotional knowledge. It would appear evolution has programmed us to: to avoid negative stimuli before seeking positive stimuli, and to avoid threats to biological survival before avoiding threats to psychological well-being. Just as animals choose to avoid fear, hunger and thirst before they seek pleasure, so, too, do we avoid threats to our physical life before we avoid threats to our quality of life.

At first glance, it looks unrealistic to ask a democracy to vote for painful changes that will make the quality of life better forty years from now at the expense of immediate gratification. We have learned, however, that we can modify human behavior to give up short-term rewards for long-term benefits through instruction, education, and environmental structures (i.e. laws and norms).

An example is cigarette smoking. When the scientific evidence became overwhelming that cigarette smoking was a leading cause of lung cancer and a liability to the national health system, opinions about cigarette smoking changed. Individuals and governments successfully sued cigarette companies, limited access to cigarettes by minors, increased their cost through taxes and reduced cigarette advertising. The result was a substantial reduction in smoking even though the individual nicotine kick was immediate and the resulting possibility of cancer decades in the future. The important point to remember is that the U.S. accomplished this reduction in cigarette smoking and lung cancer within a democratic and capitalistic framework. It never denied U.S. citizens the choice to smoke; it merely positively and negatively reinforced individuals for their choice. It positively reinforced citizens through social pressure and education for not smoking. In addition, it negatively reinforced individuals by making cigarettes more expensive, by prohibiting the sale of cigarettes to minors, by limiting cigarette advertising, by prohibiting smoking in non-smoking areas and by prosecuting those who spread false information on the dangers of smoking.

If we can clearly demonstrate that a 2.5 billion increase in the population will cause enormous harm to the quality of human life, we should be able to be equally successful in developing norms, laws and education to reduce the speed of global population growth and increase the quality of child development through similar positive and negative reinforcement. We should be able to be equally successful in reducing unwanted pregnancies without reducing the intended sexual pleasure. In addition, we should be able to achieve this goal through our existing democratic and capitalist system. We should be able to reinforce positively responsible parenting through encouragement, instruction, education, economic incentives, family planning, and free choice. Similarly, we should be able to reinforce negatively irresponsible parenting by holding both parents responsible for the economic and emotional costs required to raise children and negatively reinforcing those who try to limit family planning and free choice or who have children while they are on drugs or welfare.

We have already seen the enormous environmental damage that occurs as developing nations, with their current population, much less a 50% increase in their population, try to live like developed nations. In China, we can see the dramatic increase in pollution that comes from a rapidly developing middle class from an existing population. However, what is lacking is the scientific evidence that the psychological damage of a large population increase is equally great. What is lacking is recognition of the enormous political and economic cost to society of unintended pregnancies to poor, uneducated, and emotionally constrained parents.

This book demonstrates how to alleviate this problem. It demonstrates how our biological focus on physical survival undermines our psychological focus on mental survival. It suggests that only knowledge leads to changes in behavior that can protect us from these biological shortcomings. What we have failed to recognize is that just as there are two different ways to survive physically there are two different ways to survive mentally. We can see these two different approaches most clearly at the biological level. For the species to survive, both females and males must survive. In very simple terms, we can see that they survive in two complimentary but different ways. Biologically, women survive though their genes and through nurturing and protecting offspring. Similarly, men survive biologically through their genes, competition and impregnating females. Psychologically, the feminine approach to survival leads to empathy, equality, political democracy, beauty and for empathizing with and caring for children as well as the weaker and less fortunate. Similarly, psychologically, the masculine approach to survival leads to productivity, hierarchy, economic capitalism, and truth and respect for the most able and productive.

Our challenge is that we lack self-knowledge. Our challenge is that we tend to identify with one or the other approaches depending upon our capabilities. *In very simple terms,* if we are best at nurturing, empathy and beauty we tend to be democrats and value equality, democracy and individual rights most highly. *"In very simple terms,"* if we are best at productivity, competence and truth we tend to be republicans and value hierarchy, capitalism and responsibility most highly.

Just as we face a constant biological tension between males and females, we face a constant psychological tension between democracy and capitalism. The challenge for each of us individually and each nation collectively is to develop not only by valuing the capabilities where we are most competent but also by understanding and respecting the opposite capabilities. Our challenge is to cooperate with one another rather than to fight one another. If we are best at nurturing and affection and believe in freedom and democracy, our challenge is to recognize our biases and learn to respect competitiveness, competence, and capitalism. If we are best at competitiveness and competence and believe in responsibility and capitalism, our challenge is to recognize our biases and to learn to admire nurturing, affection and democracy. What our families, nations, and principles need to do is educate tolerance and negatively reinforce beliefs that one has the only true way to heaven and/or to right and wrong.

We cannot survive biologically without cooperation between females and males. Similarly, we cannot survive psychologically without cooperation between democracy and capitalism. Therefore, our challenge is to function as smoothly as we can within a democratic political system and a capitalist economic system. This cooperative process only works when we develop nations that structure and develop both emotional aesthetic knowledge and logical scientific knowledge. This process only works when we develop nations that elaborate <u>both</u> our need for fairness, political freedom, meaning and our drive for responsibility, competence, economic rewards and purpose. As unpopular as it may be, successful nations educate and reinforce their citizens to recognize the legitimacy of soft political and aesthetic knowledge as well as hard economic and scientific knowledge and vice versa. They educate and reinforce their citizens to recognize that while we are equal in terms of our political rights, we are unequal in terms of our economic competence. Nations can only accomplish this objective once they have developed and transmitted the necessary cerebral cortex/cooperative knowledge to minimize the effects of our reptilian egotistical knowledge. Nations can only accomplish this objective when they have developed their citizen's individual biological needs and drives into collective psychological meaning and purpose. This is an unending and all-consuming process. Ultimately, it develops egotistical behavior into cooperative behavior and cooperative behavior into contributive conduct. Ultimately, it develops the struggle for biological survival and irresponsible reproduction into the struggle for psychological survival and responsible parenting.

We can see the enormous cost of failure to develop an empathetic and educated electorate in developing nations. In these nations, there is poverty, economic corruption, and negative per capita GDP growth. In these nations, there is political unrest, social and religious violence, and civil wars.

In contrast, in the United States, however serious the different views of the different political parties, there is acceptance of majority rule and constitutional laws. An example was the Bush-Gore Presidential Election of 2000. Even though the results were highly disputed, after the Supreme Court had ruled that Bush had won, there was not only no fighting, there were not even protest demonstrations. This willingness to accept long-term rules over personal self-interests i.e. "emotional knowledge," is the critical difference between developed nations and less developed nations.

Selecting and developing knowledgeable citizens is many times more expensive and difficult than merely increasing the population. However, this selection and development is less expensive and disruptive than the Armageddon that will come from an irresponsibly reproduced and untrained larger population. Society cannot put in what irresponsible reproduction has left out. The selection and development of responsibly parented future citizens is the most important political and economic objective for any nation. The wars and devastation that will come from irresponsible reproduction will be many times greater than any natural disasters from global warming or environmental pollution.

1

HUMAN SELECTION SELECTS KNOWLEDGE

❧

"If, then, there is some end to the things we do, which we desire for its own sake (everything else being desired for the sake of this), and if we do not choose everything for the sake of something else (for at that rate the process would go on to infinity, so that our desire would be empty and vain), clearly this must be the good and the chief good. Will not the knowledge of it, then have a great influence on life? Shall we not, like archers who have a mark to aim at, be more likely to hit upon what is right?"

THE END TO THE THINGS WE DO

The end to the things we do is survival. The question is "What do we mean by survival" and "How do we survive."

Darwin has demonstrated that, biologically, the end to "the things we do" is biological survival through natural selection and reproduction.

---

1. The Basic Works of Aristotle. Random house, New York, Nicomachean Ethics, Book I Paragraph 2.

Natural selection selects functional individual behavior that increases genetic survival through biological reproduction.

Aristotle and Jesus have demonstrated that, psychologically, the end to "the things we do" is psychological survival through human selection and learning. Human selection selects functional collective behavior that increases species survival through knowledge transmission.

What has caused confusion, however, is the lack of scientific knowledge about how knowledge develops biological behavior into psychological behavior. What has caused confusion is the lack of scientific knowledge about how knowledge develops our reptilian egotism into human altruism, self-interest into enlightened self-interest, and concern for contemporary survival into concern for historical survival. We know that just as gravity is the controlling force for the movement of all inanimate objects, so, too, is survival the controlling force for the behavior of all animals, including us. Therefore, it must follow that the altruistic end to the "things we do" psychologically must develop, through knowledge, from the egotistical end of the "things we do" biologically.

Therefore, the objective of psychology is to clarify scientifically how this "survival" end of activity develops. The objective of psychology is to demonstrate:

- How our sensual instincts develop into emotional knowledge; our motor instincts into logical knowledge; and our sexual instincts into familial knowledge;
- How physical environments develop into mental environments and individual capacities into collective capabilities;
- How the objective of individual egotistical survival develops into the objective of collective cooperative survival.

- How our desire to make the world a better place for us develops into our desire to make the world a better place for others as well;
- How individuals learn knowledge and families, nations, and our species develop and transmit knowledge; And,
- How selection has changed from natural evolution and reproduction of genes in a natural environment to human development and transmission of knowledge in a human environment.

The relationships between natural selection of biological behavior through biological knowledge, and human selection of psychological behavior through psychological knowledge are dynamic. Not only does natural selection select biological behavior, but so too does biological behavior select natural environments. Primeval natural environments, as a warm mineral soup, resulted in complicated chemical chains that ultimately reproduced themselves and became life. Reproduction ultimately led to plants and animals that covered the earth and that, in turn, eventually changed the earth. This change to the earth and increased complexity of the natural environment, in turn, selected biological behavior that was more complicated.

Similarly, not only does human selection select psychological behavior, but psychological behavior develops human environments as well. Psychological behavior resulted in cooperative groups that transmitted specialized knowledge. Specialized knowledge ultimately changed the natural environment into a man-made environment that led to an explosion in the human population. The change to a man-made environment and explosion in the human population, in turn, selected collective behavior that was more complicated.

Therefore, while animal evolution is a biological process of descent with modification through the growth and reproduction of inherited capacities, human progress is a psychological process of ascent with modification through the development and transmission of acquired capabilities. As a result, we have replaced natural section of the reproductive survival of the fittest with human selection of the historical survival of the fittest.[2]

THE NATURE OF KNOWLEDGE

Knowledge consists of inherited knowledge and acquired knowledge.

Inherited knowledge consists of *historical environments* and *egotistical individual capacities.*

• *Historical environments* consist of countries, cultures, families, norms, customs, laws, roads, etc..

• *Individual capacities* consist of sexual, physical, and mental processes such as sexual orientation, sensual orientation, spatial orientation, digestion, movements, memory and thinking.

Acquired Knowledge consists of *contemporary environments and collective capabilities.*

• *Contemporary environments* consist of structures, examples, conditioning, practice, instruction education, reflection and introspection that increase collective survival.

• *Collective capabilities* consist of sexual, physical and mental values, abilities, and principles that shape collective behavior though norms, customs, laws, and concepts.

---

2. Natural and human selection select environments and capacities that increase suvival and that we are genetically programmed to use. Obviously, no one is going to stop buying food if food is available (the environment) and one can eat (the capacity). Similarly, no one is going to rub two sticks together to light a fire if one has matches (the environment) and knows how to strike a match (the capacity). Again, no one is going to walk five miles to work if one has a car (the environment) and knows how to drive a car (the capacity). And so it is with all other psychological behavior. If one has the environment and the capacity one cannot help but use them.

Knowledge results from:

- *Historical and contemporary environments* that structure coordinated *capabilities* through conditioning, example, instruction and practice.

- *Stimulated sensations* that structure coordinated *sexual responses* through sex, touching, nurturing, and grooming.

- *Conditioned movements* that structure coordinated *physical habits* through walking, running, exercise, and sports.

- *Coordinated relationships* that develop coordinated *mental skills* through practice, instruction, relationships, and organizations.

- *Reinforced emotions* that develop cooperative *family values* through affection, encouragement, recognition, praise, and responsibilities.

- *Trained logic* that develops cooperative *national abilities* through customs, laws, traditions, norms, education, and rewards. And,

- *Integrated reflections* that develop cooperative *conceptual principles* through honesty, integrity, empathy, truth, and beauty.

KNOWLEDGE DEVELOPS CAPABILITIES.

Knowledge develops capabilities that determine behaviors that increase human survival.

Defensive capabilities consist of:

- Individual defensive capabilities that defend against individual harm such as humor, values, opinions, and beliefs, and

- Collective defensive capabilities that defend against collective harm such as police, doctors, and armies.

Maintenance capabilities consist of:

- Individual maintenance capabilities that maintain individual equilibriums through play, empathy, relationships, and competence,.

- *Collective maintenance* capabilities that maintain collective equilibriums through work, norms, and laws.

Progressive capabilities consist of:

- Individual progressive capabilities that increase individual learning through practice, study, thinking, and reflecting, and
- Collective progressive capabilities that increase collective learning through parents, teachers, entrepreneurs, political leaders, artists, and scientists.

Human selection *selects* knowledge that develops capabilities and individuals; families and nations *develop* and *transmit* behavior through these capabilities. Knowledge avoids death and prolongs life in a collective environment. Knowledge, by providing meaning and purpose, makes life healthier and more pleasurable, satisfying, joyful, happy, and contented i.e. makes it more survivable. Under some circumstances, knowledge and its effect on our behavior is unclear, like the gravitational force on a meandering lowland river. Under other circumstances, knowledge and its effect on our behavior is obvious, like the gravitational force on a downward plunging mountain stream. The challenge is to clarify this "gravitational" survival force. The challenge is to clarify how individuals, families, and nations learn, transmit, and develop knowledge. The challenge is to clarify how knowledge determines how humans select one behavior and one environment over another.

THE METHODOLOGY USED TO
SUPPORT THIS THEORY

"My heart leaps up when I behold a rainbow in the sky.
So it was when a boy, so is it now I am a man. Or let me die."[3]

An explanation of human behavior requires the integration of knowledge from many disciplines—from philosophy to psychology, sociology, anthropology, computer science, and animal behavior. What is clear is that humans collectively select knowledge that teaches us, through capabilities, that our individual survival is dependent upon our interacting with others who we must learn to endure, tolerate and even love and respect. The result is that our successful individual struggle for survival is now largely dependent upon a collective struggle for survival through coordinated, cooperative, and contributive behavior

Thus, for us, the relevant factors for survival are not only biological capacities and natural environments, but also psychological capabilities and man-made environments. Moreover, because humans develop and transmit knowledge and individuals learn and apply that knowledge through capabilities, we dominate all other species.

The primary evolutionary factor contributing to the development of knowledge in humans is sex—the difference between males and females. For example, female genes from one nation are almost identical to female genes in any other nation. The same is true for male genes. However, male genes are dramatically different from female genes even within the same nation. In fact, one of the twenty-four chromosomes in males and females is different. The result is that we can easily observe different sexual organs, physical appearances, mental characteristics, family

---

3. W. Wordsworth. My Heart Leaps Up When I Behold. Francis T. Pagrave ed. 1824-1897.

relationships, and occupations between the sexes. Modern nations exaggerate these differences through make up, dress, mannerisms, and education. Therefore, while it may be difficult for males to understand males in a different nation, it is even more difficult for males to understand females, even in their own nation. Similarly, it is equally difficult for females to understand males.

As a result, just as the big bang is the primal force behind the outward movement of the universe, so too is sexual orgasm the primal force behind progressive behavior for humans. We now know scientifically that, while rainbows may make our "hearts leap up" psychologically, what makes the female "heart leap up" biologically (or pupils dilate) is babies, and what makes the male "heart leap up" biologically (or pupils dilate) is the female breast. Sex in humans is unique in that females are receptive sexually even when they cannot get pregnant. This receptivity permits a constant attraction between females and males--in females to engage in sex and nurturing in return for males providing money and protection. In addition, the resulting female need for offspring, money, and protection and male drive for competition, status, and sex develops, through knowledge, into coordinated, cooperative, and contributive (i.e. knowledgeable) relationships, love, marriage, commitment, and, ultimately, caring for all others.

Unfortunately, our struggle for psychological survival through knowledge is too complex to allow a productive discussion directly. Instead, a successful discussion can only begin with our struggle for biological survival through genes. It can only begin with the egotistical biological instincts, processes, responses, and objectives that are the basis for our altruistic psychological hardware, firmware, applications, software, and operating systems.[4]

The question remains, however, how to identify, clarify, and persuade others that our knowledge and conscious complex altruistic choices evolved and developed from genes and simple egotistical reactions. The question remains, however, how to identify, clarify, and persuade others that our developed knowledgeable choices are really choices based on an enlightened desire to prolong our life and avoid our death.

In 1809, Jean-Baptiste Lamarck, the French biologist, proposed an incorrect *Theory of Biological Evolution* in contrast to Charles Darwin's correct *Theory of Biological Evolution* fifty years later. Darwin correctly deduced that we evolved genetically from less complex animals and that natural selection causes our biological evolution. Lamarck proposed that we evolved biologically indirectly. He proposed that as our environment and habits changed they caused us to change physically. He proposed that we transferred, through reproduction, those naturally stimulated physical skills acquired during our lifetime to our offspring. An example of Lamarckism would be that if we learned to shoot a bow and arrow, we would automatically transfer that skill, through reproduction, directly to our offspring. Clearly, this is not true.

However, it would seem that Lamarck was at least partially correct. Darwin was correct about the transfer of biological genetic knowledge in a natural environment but Lamarck was correct about the transfer of

---

4. This book uses computer analogies to describe the brain's capacities and capabilities because the functioning of a computer is simpler and better understood than the functioning of our brain. **Inherited Capacities:** Our biological reptilian hardware consists of read only memory instincts such as reactions that determine our sexuality. **Acquired Capabilities:** Our psycholgical cerebreal cortex capabilities consist of firmware, applications, software and *operating systems*. *Firmware* consists of non-declarative responses that coordinate routine sensations and movements. *Applications* consist of mental non-declarative skills that weigh routine emotional interactions. *Software* consists of random access declarative memory abilities that help us execute our capabilities. *Operating systems* consist of cerebral cortex principles that evaluate, organize and apply our capabilities. *Environments* consist of our natural and curtural environments that stimulate and structure capabilities that determine our behavior.

psychological human knowledge in a collective environment. As illustrated in the example above about shooting a bow and arrow, we do not inherit the skill to shoot a bow and arrow from our parents, once they have acquired that capability. However, once our parents have acquired the knowledge to make and the skill to shoot a bow and arrow, we can inherit the physical bow and arrow. Our parents can reinforce and train us in how to make and use a bow and arrow. Finally, by creating tools like bows and arrows that survive after their death, our parents can live after death, through the development and transmission of these habits, skills, artifacts, and concepts as well as after death through their children. Thus, through man-made environments, we transfer acquired characteristics and the resulting knowledgeable behavior to subsequent generations. In addition, human selection selects us based on our ability to transmit acquired characteristics and select man-made environments just as natural selection selects animals based on their ability to reproduce inherited characteristics and select natural environments.

2

THE DEVELOPMENT OF KNOWLEDGE

❧

Nowhere have we seen change more pronounced than in our environment. During the past twenty thousand years, we have changed our environment to make it suitable--first, for hunter/gatherers, then for agrarian farmers, then for industrial nations, and most recently for a technologically integrated species. Because of these dramatically different environments, our knowledge has had to change equally dramatically. The knowledge required for being a hunter, a farmer, a manufacturer or a technologically integrated world citizen is dramatically different. If we look at the knowledge required of an aborigine in the Australian Outback or the African Desert we can see how dramatically different this knowledge is from those of a modern urban worker. Different environments stimulate and structure different functional capabilities for each environment.

In contrast, we know that while our environments have changed dramatically, we also know our genes are basically the same as they were twenty thousand years ago. Therefore, to understand how to focus on our most important problems, we have to understand where our genes provide instincts that are the most difficult to adapt to our modern world.

What we do know is that starting twenty thousand years ago, we had to structure gradually our genetic instincts in a way that permitted us to survive collectively. We had to learn to survive not just as an individual or as a family or as a group but as a city, a nation, and finally as a species. In addition, we know that in some areas we have been able to adapt our instincts to our modern world relatively easily through knowledge. This knowledge causes us to engage not only in coordinated self-interested behavior, but to engage in cooperative, mutually beneficial behavior and even altruistic contributive behavior. However, in other areas, we have been less able to develop our genetic instincts through our existing knowledge and this has led to many problems.

Therefore, if we are to understand how to avoid the Armageddon of 2054, we must first understand how we select knowledge that develops our genetic instincts for individual survival into knowledgeable capabilities for collective survival. We must understand how we develop and transmit laws, traditions, and norms that structure functional behavior that increases collective survival. To do this we must first understand how individual animal capacities evolved into collective human capabilities.

THE EVOLUTION OF
BIOLOGICAL INSTINCTS

Instincts evolved through natural environments that stimulate sensations. Instincts begin with the sensation to want to move (sensual instincts), the awareness of the direction to move (motor instincts) and the ability to move (genetic capacities). Sensation, direction, and movement in a natural environment are pervasive aspects of all behavior.

Plants cannot move—airborne seeds simply land and grow or die. Simple aquatic organisms can move. They also exist within the company of their kind but the vital energy they receive from the process of photosynthesis is of their "own" making, not taken or derived from others. Animals that are more complex have their own innate and particular absorption chemistry. Nonetheless, the manner in which they acquire food and safety increasingly involves interaction with others. Insect colonies, schools of fish, avian flocks, and animal herds illustrate the congregational aspect of interpersonal instincts that increases collective survival. However, congregational reactions within these less complex animals, despite some appearances, result in behavior that remains primarily parallel rather than coordinated. The congregational behavior is automatic. The defensive, aggressive, mating, schooling, or herding behavior at this level serves narrow functions under specific conditions. The unconscious congregational responses involved are genetically transmitted and largely irreversible. They remain virtually impervious to change through experience.

On the other hand, human selection selects congregational instincts in a man-made environment. These congregational instincts develop into sexual responses, physical habits, and mental skills through reinforcement and training. This development extends not only for the first couple of years through personal interactions but through decades of interpersonal reinforcement and training.

The question is how these complex human capabilities developed in a simple natural environment. At the earliest stages, they developed from natural environments and natural stimulation i.e. natural reinforcement and training. At the lower animal level, internal sensual and external natural stimuli acting upon an organism are as continuously various as are its reactions. They jolt it endlessly to life until it can react no more. Even in repose, the state of sleep or comatose, any animal organism is a veritable cauldron of activity. An animal's inherited chemical nature sparks and sustains its nervous as well as organic activity.

Out of an almost incalculable range of potential responses, varying animal organisms to survive disperse their energies towards some stimuli rather than others. In lower animals, we can observe automatic behavior based on instincts. For example, the simplest aquatic animal organism selects its natural environment by moving reflexively towards light in the upper layers of the ocean's waters. In these waters, natural selection selects it because of its very specific, evolutionarily selected chemical reaction to light that results in growth. In this case, natural selection selects the simplest animal organism through direct and catastrophic natural forces. Organisms lacking the sensual instinct to be attracted to light will die. Organisms lacking the directional instinct to move toward light will die. Finally, organisms lacking the motor capacity to be able to move to obtain light will also die. This primordial form of natural direct and catastrophic selection eliminates dysfunctional instincts. In sexual organisms, a similar dynamic exists. Sexual organisms lacking the sensual instinct to be attracted to the opposite sex will die. Sexual organisms lacking the directional instinct to move to the opposite sex will die. Finally sexual organisms lacking the motor capacity to move to the opposite sex will also die

THE EVOLUTION OF INDIVIDUAL KNOWLEDGE

But, clearly, in many species, there are effects of stimulation that are less catastrophic. There are effects of stimulation that do not necessarily determine life or death, but rather stimulate or repress responses in varieties of ways. They stimulate or repress responses through the positive stimulation of food, sex or warmth, and negative stimulation of injury, pain, or fear. Over time, this positive and negative stimulation subconsciously conditions a specimen's epigenetic firmware responses. This firmware consists of sensory mirror neurons and/or motor preferred neural pathways. For example, if we put our hand on a hot stove we remember the sensation (sensual information) that a hot stove causes pain. At the same time, we learn the appropriate response (directional information) to avoid putting one's hand on hot stoves. And, we learn the skill to control the movement of our hand to avoid hot stoves (motor capacity). This central nervous system firmware, in turn, determines one type of subconscious individual routines or another. However, other types of stimulation develop collective capabilities that determine how we interact with others.

COORDINATED SEXUAL RESPONSES

In the lower reaches of cellular evolution, the mechanics of natural selection started with the capacity for chemical processing of plants. It evolved into the natural selection of the capacity for genetic knowledge--inherited sensations, directed movement, and motor capacities of unisexual animals. Finally, it evolved into the natural selection of read only memory instinctive reactions in sexual animals.

Further, along the evolutionary scale, unconscious congregational reactions evolved in mammals. These congregational sexual reactions include estrogen-based and testosterone-based stimulation. This evolution of instinctive female sensual sensations and male motor movement was a critical point in the evolution of genetic knowledge. *For the first time, bisexualism introduced the dynamic of specialization.* Moreover, specialization—the basis for all complex collective behavior—resulted in different female and male genetic knowledge. The result of having different instincts for survival for female and male members within the same species and yet still enable both sexes to live together and/or copulate with one another was greater species survivability. The result for humans, *in very simple terms,* is that there are two types of genes. The first type of XX chromosome genes is for female receptive and nurturing, emotional, sensual reactions. The second type of XY chromosome genes is for male aggressive and competitive, logical motor reactions. The result is that females are the primary transmitters of what develops into emotional sensual knowledge and males are the primary transmitters of what develops into logical motor knowledge. More important, it is not that our emotional knowledge is not logical. Rather when we apply emotional knowledge, we apply our logic to our internal sensual information and feelings. Similarly, it is not that logical knowledge is not emotional. Rather when we apply logical knowledge, we apply our emotions to our external motor information and reasoning.

Coordinated congregational reactions mean mutually beneficial reactions for males and females. We can see the importance of sexual differences and mutually beneficial reactions by imaging a world of all males or all females. Obviously, this world could not survive biologically because it could not reproduce. Even more important, it would be a world that could not survive psychologically. It is only from female receptivity, nurturing, and beauty that we learn about *meaning* and the ability to survive through helping others *to want to live*. Similarly, it is only from male aggressiveness, competitiveness, and truth that we learn about *purpose* and the ability to survive through helping others *to be able to live*. That is why in single parent households it is so difficult to provide examples of both female and male role models. This shortcoming of not having the example of how the opposite sexes can provide different specialized roles and yet live harmoniously together is critical. If the family does not provide the emotional example of the opposite sexes living together, society cannot replace that shortcoming. Furthermore, because our genes have not changed in twenty million years, our sexual instincts are programmed to peak in our early teens, which was appropriate when our life expectancy was twenty-five: there was a chance our species would be extinct; and it took less than a decade to learn all we needed to survive. Today, however, our life expectancy is closer to seventy-five, our danger is over population not extinction and it takes over two decades to learn what we need to survive.

*"We hold these truths to be self-evident – that all men are created equal.
That they are endowed by their creator with certain inalienable rights,
including the rights to life, liberty, and the pursuit of happiness."*[5]

5, The Declaration of Independence.

Feelings are an individual's unique emotional knowledge. Feelings develop from reinforced family sensations. While the Declaration of Independence proclaims universal feelings for "life, liberty, and the pursuit of happiness," environments and feelings are different for each individual, family, and nation. Therefore, since what makes us feel happy is different for each individual, our right to the pursuit of happiness must include our right to free choice of our own unique pursuit. Since free choice is the critical element of the pursuit of happiness, the Declaration of Independence ought to have read "... the rights to life, liberty, and the pursuit of happiness *through individual free choice.*"

In contrast, reasoning applies to external information. Reasoning develops from trained logic. Therefore, while some reasoning is different for each individual, most reasoning is universal.

As a result, *individual emotional knowledge* is different for each individual but at the same time, it must take into account *collective emotional knowledge* though self-knowledge. Therefore, it is more difficult to transmit emotional knowledge to the next generation than it is to transmit logical knowledge. That is why, in a democracy, we make the mistake of believing "beauty" is *only* in the eye of the beholder rather than an objective *collective* standard as well. This is why in a democracy it is so difficult to see the psychological effects of a 33% increase in the global population. Conversely, we see "truth" as more objective as in our example of an asteroid. One can explain most economic and political cycles by the lag time in transmitting emotional knowledge as it tries to catch up with rapid progress in logical knowledge. For example, we can reason the letter of a law such as in Title 9 or "All men and women are equal before the law," more easily than we can feel tolerance, respect, admiration, and love for all men and women. Similarly, we can reason how to use a computer more rapidly than we can feel the desire to use a computer for the welfare of others as well as ourselves.

COORDINATED PHYSICAL HABITS

Among the most complex mammals, there is the subconscious female selection of estrogen- based nurturing habits that are an extension of instinctive female receptivity. Similarly, there is the subconscious male selection of testosterone based competitive habits that are an extension of instinctive male aggression.

These acquired coordinated emotional and logical firmware-based habits result in specialized characteristics. Within groups of mammals, collective mirror neurons and preferred neural pathways allow for substantial differences in male and female physical habits to coexist. At the same time, these differences tend to stimulate responses between the sexes that result in coordinated behavior.

Even so far down the evolutionary scale as birds, the important energizing and protective family habits of a male and female family unit are evident. These reactions and responses become more complex among species with still longer, more varied maturational phases. All through the mammalian world are unending examples of individual females engaged in the feeding and affectionate nurturing of their offspring. Similarly, all through the mammalian world are unending examples of individual males engaged in competing for females and maintaining hierarchies that can protect the family group.

Nurturing and a safe environment result in the sub-conscious interactions and the resulting stimulation and motor conditioning that comes from grooming, vocalizing, touching, and demonstrating functional habits to offspring. This female nurturing and male protective behavior, in turn frees the offspring's energy resources so that it can devote the time to "play." Through play, offspring can learn habits with their siblings without having to expend energy-gathering food, and/or avoiding danger. Furthermore, families and groups reduce the need to develop through trial and error. Conditioned (i.e. stimulated and demonstrated habits) transmit knowledge and reduce the energy required for the young to learn and accelerate development.

These interactions are a key part of emotional development. Single parent families lack examples of both the female nurturing and the male protector roles. This deficiency results in a shortcoming in child development. Unfortunately, no well-meaning "No Child Left Behind" programs will ever be able to make up this family learned sexual knowledge.

Furthermore, it is not difficult to see how, over time, the processes of family interaction have oriented the more complex mammals towards extended nurturing and defensive units. It is not difficult to see how these extended nurture units, in turn, have resulted in conditioned group formations. These formations facilitate group activities for guarding of the young, obtaining food, and defending the group. As has been said, receptive and aggressive habits that result in nursing and mating are due to largely conditioned physical movements. However, they do anticipate flexible coordinated relationships that determine, within primate groups, the specialized individual behavior that aids in the survival of others *including non-family members.*

COORDINATED MENTAL SKILLS

This is an important point in the development of knowledge. When the members of a group reach the conscious skills to aid in the survival of others, not only within, but also beyond family units, the types of coordinated skills expands. They expand to include mutually beneficial specialized mental skills for each individual within a group. They develop from integrated group interactions. The capacity of interpersonal family environments and stimulation to contribute to survival attracts to it the same pressures of natural selection of individual genes that operate on lower animals. In contrast, the extra-familial conditioning of individual specialized mental skills can protect and energize genetically diverse members that could not have survived without the contributions of other members of the group. In the spiraling chain of exchanging benefits, the types of collective skills expand to include specialized skills of non-family members as well as family members.

In addition, it is not difficult to see how these coordinated relationships among primates have evolved and expanded to play an increasing part in these groups struggle for survival. Similarly, it is not difficult to see how this group selection of specialized skills in mammals has expanded to include the human selection of knowledge that stimulates, structures, develops, and transmits specialized individual capabilities.

The primate transfer of responses and habits discussed above is through example and mimicry. The responses and habits are subconscious and are inseparable from the interactions. In primitive humans, however, we can observe consciously reinforced and trained mental skills and artifacts. The resulting skills lead to unique behavior for each individual. For example, we encourage and instruct boys and girls to become aware of their differences and value their own skills. Females are encouraged and instructed to take gratification from nurturing skills. In the same way, males are encouraged and instructed to take gratification from competitive skills. Development of nurturing and competitive skills results in self-knowledge about one's position in different environments based on one's own sexual orientation and skills.

Since we acquire, rather than inherit, these skills, we can develop masculine or feminine skills regardless of sex depending upon our personal capacities and experience. In other words, females that can only biologically be bearers and nurturers of offspring can acquire logical skills and psychologically become lawyers, accountants, scientists, and the aggressive, competitive team player or spouse. Similarly, males that biologically can only be aggressive hunter/providers can acquire emotional skills and psychologically become poets, musicians, artists, and the receptive, nurturing family oriented spouse. The most important point, however, is that emotional skills, *at their most basic level*, evolve and develop from female estrogen-based receptive nursing, gathering and nurturing responses. Similarly, logical skills, *at their most basic level*, evolve and develop from male testosterone-based hierarchical, one-point perspective motor and competitive responses.

THE EVOLUTION OF COLLECTIVE KNOWLEDGE

This is a second critical point in the development of knowledge. When humans reached the mental capacity to not only interact through physical habits, but to cooperate through mental skills, a new level of development occurs. At this level of development, individuals became able to not only value and consciously practice and develop their own specialized skills, but to admire and respect the specialized skills of others. By practicing and developing individual specialized skills, the variability of individual genes increases.

Thus, female nurturing and male competitive reactions lead to differing personal feelings and reasoning. As a result, each individual because of his/her environment and experience develops unique self-knowledge. This self-knowledge shapes, for each individual, unique appropriate cooperative behavior. It permits humans to expand the process of choosing one behavior over another based upon unique cooperative capabilities rather than on just coordinated responses and habits.

COOPERATIVE FAMILY VALUES

Cooperative female family values develop from reinforced family emotions and pleasurable family stimulation such as nursing, touching, talking, and interacting and result in loving relationships and family norms. Similarly, cooperative male family values develop from logical competitive family stimulation and practiced movements such as play, competition, and aggression and result in family morals. Norms and morals lead to unique values within the family depending upon each individual's unique capacities whether for gathering and nurturing or hunting and providing. Again, single parent families are lacking the necessary cooperative role models for <u>both</u> sexes.

However, even for two parent families, the limitations of family and group values are the lack of flexibility. Family encouragement and instruction only develop "cooperative" values within a family unit. They only develop capabilities that are relevant for specific families and family situations. The limitation of family encouragement and instruction is that it permits limited tolerance and adaptability with regard to other family or group values. An example of the lack of flexibility associated with family values occurs in religious families and tribes. These religious families and tribes place great emphasis on tribal loyalties and traditions. Group hierarchies and prayer emphasize the memorized wisdom of past inspirational leaders rather than analyzed current information and knowledge. In addition, in nations where there is a reliance on a pictorial written language, learning the language requires an extra two years of schooling. More important than the extra two years of language schooling, however, is the resulting attraction to like-minded individuals and families due to the reliance on instruction and "memorization." This emphasis on instruction and "kind and unkind" and "right and wrong" behavior in turn, leads to increased emphasis on remembering. The result is that social/religious families, tribes, and pictorial language nations often value remembered traditional knowledge more than analyzed current knowledge. As a result, their adaptability is limited. Only when they have developed political and economic knowledge can they progress to a functional nation.

In addition, families and religion only focuses on one-half of knowledge--the attempt to find meaning. When Jesus says, "Render unto Caesar those things that belong to Caesar; render unto God those things that belong to God" or "Do unto others as you would have them do unto you" he makes an excellent case for half of the "end of the things we do"--that is, for a way to find personal emotional meaning. **In very simple terms,** it is what democracy is about.

However, Jesus never discusses how Caesar should behave or how capitalism works. The other half of "the end of the things we do" has to do with how we are able to survive in a competitive world. For example, "do unto others as you would have them do unto you" is not a sufficient guide for dealing with a Nazi Germany or terrorists. Nor is the Beatles refrain "All you need is love" a sufficient guide for making a living.

In contrast, there is also a logical struggle for interpersonal purpose in a competitive world. For example, Vince Lombardi's "Winning is not the most important thing, it is the only thing" or the Wall Street Golden Rule "He who has the gold rules" may be sufficient guidelines for football or capitalism. They make an excellent case for half of the "end of the things we do"--the way to find purpose. **In very simple terms,** it is what capitalism is about. However, capitalism alone does not provide a sufficient guide for dealing with a wife or children.

COOPERATIVE NATIONAL ABILITIES

Cooperative national abilities develop from trained logic. For satisfied and encouraged individuals, the memory of past reinforcement leads to empathy and respect for others as well as competent routines and abilities. In other words, valuing the milk of human nursing and sensual capabilities ultimately progresses to values emphasizing the milk of human kindness or emotional capabilities. Similarly, for practiced and instructed individuals, the memory of past hierarchical training leads to ethical routines and capabilities. In other words, the memory of past fair family cooperation and logical capabilities ultimately leads to the concern for progressive taxation and just laws. The application of these abilities through work and cooperation develops an appreciation for the values, abilities, and principles of others. As a result, developed nations reward productive occupations and educate cooperative opinions in order to survive. In so doing, they place a greater emphasis on freedom of, and tolerance for, different feelings and thoughts. National survival and the need for more complicated mutually beneficial cooperative choices involve more flexible methodologies than the application of single-family values or past beliefs. Nations use impersonal rewards (such as money) to motivate competent work. They use education (in schools and universities) to clarify ethical cooperation and inspire specialized abilities. As a result, modern nations select productive, fair, environments through elections, majority opinions, organizations, check and balance systems, and laws. Instead of black and white commandments, like "thou shalt not kill"," applicable as a simple guide for family or tribal values, a Court opinion on the death penalty is required to select behavior consistent with just laws.

This is a third critical point in the development of cooperative capabilities. The importance of acquired capabilities relative to inherited capacities increases dramatically when humans, through nations, develop productive economic and fair political environments. The compensating strengths of complex, intergenerational, and familial/group encouragement of norms and instruction of morals provides protection and energizes genetically diverse members that could not have survived without the cooperation of others. However, the energy released by rewarded work and reinforced cooperation exponentially increase the willingness of diverse citizens to contribute to the survival of others because of their specialized capabilities. In the spiraling chain of mutually beneficial behavior, dramatically diversified citizens increase a nation's economic and political success as a whole by providing widely varied specialized capabilities. These diversified citizens cooperate not only because they were encouraged and instructed by their families but because they were rewarded and educated by their country.

COOPERATIVE CONCEPTUAL PRINCIPLES

Cooperative conceptual principles develop from integrated reflection. For a few, past reinforcement leads to insight on how to inspire others through encouragement and beauty. Similarly, past training leads to reflections on how to motivate others through education and truth. This conceptual stage of development for humans comes from cognition-- from not only externally reinforced and rewarded individual capabilities but from internally reinforced introspective and reflective principles. These principles result in psychic rewards and psychic education. In other words, reflecting on past reinforcement inspires psychic insights. Similarly, reflecting on past training reveals psychic reflections. As our occupations and capabilities become more specialized, only we know how we can best contribute to the welfare of others. Only we know how best to apply our own capabilities and how to maximize our pursuit of happiness. Only we know how we can obtain the most reinforcement and rewards. In addition, we obtain meaning from the freedom to make that choice and a sense of purpose from making that choice.

The relatively narrow range of selection of behavior for the many develops for the few into an infinitely wide range of contributive choices. In order to expand the capacity for self-knowledge, democratic nations extend reinforcement and training to include adult insights, reflections, as well as artistic and scientific creativity. Instead of just "testaments" and "commandments," modern nations use literature, constitutions, democracy, capitalism, truth, and beauty to shape, clarify, and develop the capabilities necessary for common survival and progress in a complex world. Instead of just externally reinforced and trained laws and regulations, modern nations also inspire and motivate internally reinforced and trained creativity.

THE DEVELOPMENT OF FUNCTIONAL ENVIRONMENTS

The way to increase functional behavior is to develop functional environments that impersonally stimulate (i.e. unconsciously and subconsciously structure) functional capabilities. The result is, that in modern democratic, capitalistic nations, a selection of common individual, family, national, and global behavior has developed that transmits aesthetic and just environments. These nations transmit artistic and scientific knowledge that promotes life, prosperity, freedom, and dignity and reduces illness, death, prejudice, and intolerance. This common mutually beneficial behavior leads to specialized professions and leaders. It also leads to check and balance systems. These check and balance systems provide external reinforcement and training to the many individuals in need of inspiration and lacking in motivation. These check and balance systems include:

- The family and national check and balance systems of balancing traditional instruction with universal education;
- The social check and balance system of balancing friendship with impersonal rights;

- The legal check and balance system of balancing individual freedoms with collective responsibilities;
- The political check and balance system of balancing democratic fairness and capitalistic discipline;
- The constitutional check and balance system of balancing the whims of a democratic electorate with the counterbalancing powers of the President, the Congress, the Courts, and a Constitution;
- The economic check and balance systems of balancing the excesses of competitive capitalism with the counterbalancing powers of the boards of directors, accountants, management, and economic laws and regulations. And finally and most important,
- The sexual check and balance system of balancing emotional knowledge and the desire to survive through pleasure, tolerance, and freedom with logical knowledge and the ability to survive through parental responsibility, and competition.

In nations like the United States, human selection transmits capabilities that result in not only political democracy, but economic capitalism, as well. In these nations, each citizen votes not only with their ballots but also with their feet, time, energy, and dollars. They vote not only for their leaders, but for their friends, churches, and expenditures as well. In their pursuit of happiness, governments give as much "choice" as possible as long as it does not harm others including the choice to live or die or to have or not have a child.

As a result, in democratic, capitalistic nations, selection forces require individuals constantly to develop individual routines and collective capabilities. Some development results from sexual stimulation and individual responses. Some development results from individual physical stimulation and individual habits. Some development results from mental stimulation and individual skills. Some development results from family stimulation and collective values. Some development results from national stimulation and collective abilities. Finally, some development results from conceptual stimulation and collective principles.

These human selection forces, at their most complex level, develop capabilities and nations that transmit not only externally reinforced cooperative behavior but also internally reinforced contributive behavior. Moreover, in a world of exchanging benefits, by choosing behavior that increases our capabilities and improves our nations, we increase the development and survival of ourselves, our nation, other nations, and ultimately the dominance of our species.

3

KNOWLEDGE DEVELOPS CAPABILITIES

I*n ancient Greece every four years, there was an archery contest. The organizers selected the best archers from all over the country and after a series of contests reduced the number of contestants to the final four best archers. The Greeks held the final contest in the harbor in Athens in front of an enormous crowd. The organizers of the contest tied a pigeon with a string to the top of the mast of the tallest ship. Each archer in turn shot at the pigeon. The first archer shot an arrow that stuck in the mast only a few inches below the pigeon. The crowd cheered with delight at such a fine shot. The second archer shot his arrow and severed the string that tied the pigeon to the mast. The crowd gasped in amazement. The third archer fired his arrow at the pigeon*

43

as it circled high in the sky above the ship and shot it out of the air. The crowd roared with approval. The fourth archer drew his bow back and fired his arrow high into the sky. Only those standing near the fourth archer could hear him exclaim, "I shoot for the gods to see."[6]

Just as natural selection has selected us to grow individually through instincts, so too has human selection selected us to develop collectively through knowledge. The challenge, however, is to describe how our individual coordinated capabilities expanded to include collective contributive capabilities. The challenge is to describe how behavior develops in order to increase the survival of others at what appears to be our own expense or behavior that is "for the gods to see." We can best answer that question by tracing how capabilities developed.

THE DEVELOPMENT OF GENETIC CAPABILITIES

Individual capabilities result from stimulated genetic reactions and conditioned genetic responses. For example, at the internal sensual level (such as the drive for thirst), our emotional valuation component compares the internal sensual input (the random access memory actual shape of our blood cells) with the genetic logical constant (the read only memory ideal rounded shape of our blood cells) to see if action is necessary. If action is necessary and our cells are misshapen, we feel the sensation of thirst. We have no choice. Once our cells are misshapen, we must feel thirst or we will die.

Similarly, at the motor level (such as in movements to obtain water), our central processing unit component compares the external vision input (visual stimuli) with an assessment of the distance to an object using one

---

point perspective. We have no choice. If we are thirsty, we must use the logic of one point perspective to move to find water or we will die.

Furthermore, our environment also structures preferred neural pathways to focus past information and use that information to adjust and refine reactions into functional subconscious sensual and motor responses. For example, pleasurable internal sensations from drinking water when we are thirsty and the memory of past pleasurable sensations from drinking water when we are thirsty conditions responses to obtain future stimulation (pleasurable internal sensations) from moving to drink water. Similarly, external motor injuries and the memory of past motor injuries provide memories that condition responses to avoid future injuries (motor external logic).

This process of comparing inherited constants and remembered information with short-term sensual stimulation and motor memories and responding to the comparison helps explain our more rudimentary routines. It explains behavior when stimuli result in the feeling of thirst when our blood cells are misshapen and cold when our blood temperature is below 98.6°, hunger when our blood sugar is too low, and fear when there is danger. Because of sensual stimuli, our lower brain comparators detect changes from sensual constants that result in feelings. These biological sensual comparators then activate and prioritize motor responses that we think are most likely to correct disequilibrium. Our genes provide the constants that result in the feelings that identify disequilibrium and the reasoning that directs us to move to make the corrections.

At the hardware level, genes also transmit other emotional standards or internal biological sensual constants such as sex (female and male), harmony (pitch--multiples of vibrations per minute), tempo (fast or slow relative to our heartbeat), rhythm (repetitions of 3/4 and 4/4 timing, etc.), and smoothness (the female breast and a baby's skin). The awareness of sensual biological constants such as the shape of our blood cells or our blood temperature motivates our drive for emotional psychological constants such as kindness, empathy, love, and beauty.

Similarly, at the hardware level, genes also transmit other external environmental standards or logical constants such as assessments of temperature (hot and cold), distance (near and far), and time (today and tomorrow). The awareness of biological constants about temperature, movement, and time inspires our drive for psychological reasoning about fairness, competence, morality, ethics, and truth.

At the applications level, the valuation component compares the anticipated expenditure of energy with our perception of the value of the anticipated reward to evaluate our choices. For example, we evaluate our choices on whether or not we play to make us feel like we want to live or whether or not we work to enable us to live. Our operating system component and our genes provide the drives that motivate work and the needs that inspire play.

In addition, at the conceptual level, such as in activity strategies to integrate these constants, the valuation component compares the choice and our memory of past choices to select the most survivable choice.

This framework explains conscious mental activity when inner stimuli register and develop internal drives. In addition, it explains conscious mental activity that results from external stimuli that trigger and develop internal drives. Internal and external stimuli, memories of ideal psychological values, and operating system comparators detect changes from ideal emotional and logical standards. These comparisons trigger operating systems that select choices we feel and reason are most likely to avoid death, correct disequilibrium, or prolong life. Psychological operating systems seek pleasure if we are in pain, health, if we are sick, honesty if we are confused, affection, if we are lonely, working if we are in need of money, obeying the law if we are in fear of punishment, and meaning and purpose if we have energy left over.

THE DEVELOPMENT OF COLLECTIVE COOPERATIVE CAPABILITIES

The psychological basis for cooperative behavior seems self-evident. Once we learn to identify ourselves from someone else and be around one another, by definition, we learn to engage in cooperative behavior. If someone else has the capacity to do something easily that is difficult for us, but easy for him, we will choose to benefit from his comparative advantage. For example, in the case of chimpanzees, I will groom you if you will groom me. Alternatively, for humans, I will scratch your back if you will scratch mine. In modern societies, we have extended this concept of scratching someone's back to paying them money. I will work for you if you pay me money and I will pay you money if you work for me.

The question remains however, as to how cooperative behavior evolved and developed into contributive behavior. A simple example of capabilities is competent physical movement. If we use the example of a pilot crashed in the middle of a desert, we can imagine different levels of knowledge about his attempts to return to safety. If he does not know where he is, he will probably wander aimlessly in any direction. If he knows approximately where he is, he will use the sun as his guide and head off in the approximate direction in which he thinks he should be headed. If he has a Global Positioning System (GPS), knows how long his water will last, and how far he has to go, he can determine the direction to head, measure his distance, know how much water he can drink each day and how many miles he must travel each day to reach safety.

Therefore, capabilities enable behavior with a GPS and a map whose objective is long-term survival. It is behavior based on knowing the right thing to do for the right reason (i.e. because it increases our desire and ability to survive). Therefore, our challenge is to have a SPS system (Survival Positioning System) that integrates where we are, the direction to head, the best way to survive in any circumstance or location and in any unit of survival.

Our efforts to survive, *at the most complex level,* result in the attempt to survive after death. Historical efforts to survive after death started with efforts to survive physically after death through mummification like the Egyptians. They expanded to include efforts to survive after death through:

 great deeds (the Greeks),

 great works (the Romans),

 offspring (monarchies)

 heaven (religions) and finally,

 knowledge (historical contributions).

History and science have demonstrated the limitations of many of the previous attempts at life after death. Instead, history suggests that most of us can only successfully survive after death through our children and through capabilities—through contributions to our environment and to others that live on after our death.

Most behavior deals with engaging in the right behavior (mutually beneficial behavior) for the wrong reason (learned behavior) as opposed to engaging in the right contributive behavior for the right reason (understood behavior). Most behavior deals with doing the right thing because our genes, our environment, our body, family, friends, employers, and nations negatively reinforce us if we select the wrong behavior. And, this instinctive, stimulated, structured, and transmitted behavior covers the vast majority of our behavior. Once we internalize the right direction to steer without the need for external reinforcement or training, or once we have developed our own internalized Suvival Positioning System, we are able to maximize our unique capabilities, to not only cooperate with, but to contribute to others. The basis for this SPS occurs through lthe family. If the family does not structure, train and instruct an SPS for their children, society cannot develop one for them.

Meaningful and purposeful knowledge combined (or self-knowledge) is the knowledge that enables us to maximize our strengths and avoid our weaknesses. However, much of the progress of modern society has resulted from developing ways to shape behavior to make it "contributive," even if we engage in the behavior for the money or praise rather than because we feel and reason that it contributes to others. Modern societies develop behavior through cultures--through historical environments and individual, family, national, and conceptual knowledge. This knowledge encourages mutually beneficial capabilities by making it difficult to avoid punishment if we engage in self-interested behavior. Because of our lack of understanding due to insufficient parental training, we often choose to act in the interest of others for the wrong reason. For example:

• To negotiate with our spouse or significant other for as much sex as we can get for as little money as possible, or to negotiate for as much money as possible for as little sex as possible (mutually beneficial behavior), rather than giving as much as we are able to with love, without regard for return (altruistic behavior);

- To be polite to powerful or wealthy people to avoid conflict or to feel important or to contribute to charity only because that earns tax deductions and social praise (mutually beneficial behavior), rather than being polite and generous to all people because it is helpful to others (altruistic behavior);

- To do unto others as we would have them do unto us only because we believe that will lead to a better life after death in heaven (mutually beneficial behavior), rather than because that is the way to find meaning and purpose in life (altruistic behavior);

- To obtain as much money as we can for as little effort as possible (mutually beneficial behavior), rather than engage in the most contributive work we are able, even if it pays less money (altruistic behavior);

- To pay as few taxes as possible without being prosecuted (mutually beneficial behavior), rather than paying the fair amount of taxes, because it is just (altruistic behavior);

- To obey the speed limit, join the army or serve on jury duty only because we will be punished if we don't (mutually beneficial behavior), rather than because it is our responsibility (altruistic behavior); and

- To discover or create something new only because it will be recognized or profitable (mutually beneficial behavior), rather than because it increases human survival (altruistic behavior).

In short, most behavior is the result of a combination of incentives, internal and external. The closer a behavior is to altruistic behavior the more it is engaged in because it is "right," because it promotes life and avoids death rather than because it results in positive external reinforcement or even in spite of the fact that it results in negative external reinforcement.

The more a capability is engaged in because it is "right" the less it becomes explainable to others. In a democracy, most of us are highly suspicious of anyone who does anything for reasons other than pleasure, gratification, encouragement, rewards, praise, or recognition. Most of us are used to externally reinforced "behavior" and skeptical of anyone so egotistical and un-egalitarian that he/she talks about "internally reinforced altruistic behavior" based on insights and reflections. We are taught on Sesame Street to "Do what you want to do/Be what you want to be/Believe in yourself." And this is as it should be. In a democracy like the United States, it is necessary to break down concepts like "justice" and "liberty" so they are clear to the young and inexperienced. Therefore, as families we instruct our children to be open and polite to others as if it was natural to be kind and loving for the wrong reason, because they will be criticized and punished if they are not open and polite. Similarly, as nations we institute laws and regulations to force the young and inexperienced to behave as if it was natural to be just and fair, for the wrong reason--because they will be punished if they are not just and fair. The result is that those who pursue contributive altruistic behavior learn quickly to hide their true motives and discuss them only with friends or groups with similar feelings, values and beliefs. Instead, if they are to fight for what they know is true and just, they must do so though knowledge, through facts and experiences that clarify meaningful and purposeful behavior.

Princeton's "It is better to serve than be served," Christ's "Do unto others what you would have them do unto you," Saulk's polio vaccine, Watson's and Cricks theory of DNA, and Kennedy's "Ask not what your country can do for you but what you can do for your country" are the best definitions of altruistic behavior. By definition, we cannot defend our altruistic behavior; altruistic behavior provides its own psychic rewards. As an individual, if we feel we have to defend or explain why we did what was right, then we have not understood the nature of altruistic behavior. The whole point of contributive altruistic behavior is to be helpful to others in the long term even though they do not understand or reject the contributions in the short run.

Altruistic behavior or "conduct," therefore, is meaningful and purposeful behavior for a particular individual, at a particular place, at a particular time, with a particular set of capabilities. It is doing the right thing for the right reason because it promotes life and avoids death--not because it is stimulated, satisfying, encouraged or rewarded. It is doing the right thing that contributes to the suvival of others even though it is negatively reinforced or ignored by others. It is not a universal conduct, with a capital C, applicable for everyone all the time. Instead, it varies dramatically from location to location, individual-to-individual, family-to-family, nation-to-nation, and historical period to historical period.

In short, conduct is inspiring and clarifying; it is generosity without the expectation and even the need for reinforcement and training from others. It is behavior that is entirely personal. Only we know about our behavior's purpose and even if we/she try to explain, others, with a less complex understanding of self -interest, will twist the purpose of our conduct into some more self-serving form of behavior. They will say the behavior was done for economic rewards, political parisanship, or self agrandizement rather than for making the world a better place in which to live. Furthermore, conduct occurs most frequently in countries where there are democratic freedoms and capital markets where citizens can can afford to learn from their mistakes. In market based, participatory democracies, citizens have the luxury of being able to satisfy their basic needs for food, warmth, safety, relationships, traditions, freedom, and dignity. They conclude what is right from their own cognition, not just because of external reinforcement and training, and this learning process requires energy, time, money, insights, and reflection.

The result in modern societies is a democratization of altruistic behavior through the freedom of individual choice. Each individual decides how to best contribute to making the world a better place for him/herself and for others--whether that better place is due to how we develop as an individual, raise our children, work in our occupations, serve our country, or contribute to human knowledge. The development of values and beliefs has developed in modern nations into the development of participation and understanding through democratic elections and market disciplined approaches to problem solving rather than elitist and regulatory approaches. It has developed into democratic and market check and balance systems to integrate and train citizens with a less complex understanding of self-interest. These check and balance systems develop our genetically programmed and humanly selected instincts to choose pleasure over pain, health over illness, positive beliefs over negative beliefs, prosperity over poverty, right over wrong, legality over illegality, progress over tradition, truth over falsehood, and beauty over ugliness.

THE UNIQUENESS OF INDIVIDUAL AND COLLECTIVE CAPABILITIES

A number of factors including our unique genes, physical environment, reinforcement, and training affect the speed at which we learn and the way in which we learn. Our genes determine our mental capacities and provide the basis for learning. Our environment determines behavior and accelerates learning though stimulated and structured capabilities. Our experience from cultures, interactions, reinforcement, and training develops our capabilities and determines the complexity of choices available to us.

Altruistic behavior is complex because it results from integrating environments, feeling, reasoning, and capabilities, i.e. integrating emotion and logic and applying that emotion and logic effectively in each specific environment. We must not only know what is contributive but also develop the self-knowledge to know how we are most able to contribute and how we are most likely to feel we want to contribute. Therefore, the greatest challenge we face is to feel like surviving and knowing how to survive in spite of a lack of external reinforcement or even in spite of negative external reinforcement. The greatest challenge we face is to be able to contribute to others while at the same time recognizing and respecting the contributions of others. We can be successful in achieving this balancing act for two reasons.

• The first reason is occupational and emotional *comparative advantage*.

• The second reason is the ability to survive at *different levels of complexity*.

Comparative Advantage: In whatever occupation we choose, there will be others who could be better at our occupation than we are. If we are a janitor there will be neurosurgeons, lawyers, bankers or others who could be better janitors than we are. However, since a nation needs citizens for many different occupations, our objective is to find the occupation that best uses our capabilities. Democratic nations reward, respect, and admire each citizen for what he/she can contribute and allow each citizen to obtain his/her own unique meaning and purpose. In contrast, dictatorial nations focus the vast majority of the rewards, respect, and admiration on the most competitive, powerful, wealthy, or talented. This is why democracies are so powerful, since they are able to inspire and motivate an entire population rather than just a few.

Similarly, whatever our family role, there will be others that are better fathers or mothers, husbands or wives, daughters or sons than we are in our families. However, since each family is unique, what matters to our family is how we behave in our family as a father, mother, husband, wife, daughter, or son, not how others behave in other families.

Different Levels of Complexity: There are also different levels of emotional, logical, and environmental complexity. When a mother plays peek-a-boo with her baby, the baby at first feels and reasons and therefore "knows" that the mother has gone away when she hides her face behind a pillow. Eventually, the baby learns the mother is still there when she hides behind a pillow, and the initial delight in re-seeing the mother is discontinued because the baby "knows" that just because the mother is out of sight does not mean she is not there.

In our life, as we mature and learn, many issues are equally confusing. We find we "know" with different degrees of certainty. Our judicial system illustrates this point. For civil cases, we "know" and can make a decision when there is a preponderance of evidence. For criminal cases, we "know" and can make a decision when there is evidence "beyond a reasonable doubt." In addition, in our legal system, we are never expected to "know" "beyond all doubt." In contrast, artistically and scientifically we are able to "know" i.e. understand "beyond all doubt."

There are, however, many different concepts in our lives that we "know" only gradually or perhaps not at all depending upon our environment and development. Examples are the existence of Santa Claus, the importance of reinforcement and motivation, the importance of training and clarification, the belief in a God or Heaven, the belief that man evolved, or was divinely created, or the knowledge of human principles of right and wrong. In each case, we go through stages of knowing depending upon our environment and development. When we are confused or uncertain about the answers to these questions, our degree of certainty affects the energy and consistency of our choices.

Politicians, for example, take into account varying levels of capabilities in their electorate and take their stand on issues that are politically feasible. However, politicians also recognize that, as Abraham Lincoln said, "you can fool all of the people some of the time and some of the people all of the time but you cannot fool all of the people all of the time." Furthermore, even if one could fool most of the people during a lifetime, like Stalin, history demonstrates that you will not be able to fool most of the people after one's lifetime.

As a result, and as we develop, we increase our ability to survive and avoid death by expending as much energy as possible toward progressive ends as we perceive them, and as little energy as possible toward maintenance and defensive ends. Just as our body must devote its energy first to cure illness and injury, we too must obtain sex, food, health, safety, confidence, and only then devote energy to development. This prioritization is true whether the energy is motor energy or time, emotional energy or attention, social energy or praise, traditional energy or help, economic energy or money, political energy or due process, aesthetic energy or beauty, or principled energy, or truth. Our personal circumstances, genes and environment determine the energy available for our activity. Expressed another way, we devote our energies to sexual pleasure, physical health, mental satisfaction, family joy, and national success before we devote our energies to conceptual principles. Once we have achieved pleasure, health, satisfaction, joy, and success, however, we have no choice but to devote our remaining energies to achieving contentment from meaning and purpose.

Therefore, we must use our operating systems to sequence, prioritize, analyze, integrate, and apply our capabilities. For example, if one feels and reasons but does not understand that is not knowledge. To feel what is beautiful (to be mature and to feel a standard) and to reason what is true (to be competent and know how to use a process) is different from to feel and to know and therefore to pursue energetically what is beautiful and true. To purse energetically what is beautiful and true we must use our reinforced feelings to motivate and our trained reasoning to clarify our choices most effectively in our specific environment.

However, we also learn to endure "disequilibrium" resulting in defensive development that helps us live with hunger, cold, illness, injury, pain, fear, and confusion. These defensive equilibriums result in our maturation, our "focusing on" positive reinforcement and mitigating, rationalizing, avoiding, or coping with negative reinforcement. In other words, as well as being praised and rewarded, we are also criticized and punished. As well as feeling well, fit, and confident, we are sometimes ill or made to feel insecure by others. Defensive development helps us endure, tolerate, and adjust to such disequilibrium and still be able to survive.

Thus, in order to survive, we mature through self-knowledge. Each of us, individually, develop the capability to integrate our unique defensive, maintenance, and progressive capabilities through values, beliefs, opinions, and reflections that extend our range of choices by permitting us to adapt to our environment. As a result, the struggle to survive physically and avoid biological injury or death has evolved to the struggle to survive mentally and avoid psychological injury or death. In addition, the majority of our individual activity is devoted to defending and maintaining as well as developing our psychological health.

4

CAPABILITIES DETERMINE BEHAVIOR

❦

Capabilities determine three types of biological behavior—homeogretic behavior, homeostatic behavior and homeorhetic behavior. These three types of biological behavior are the basis for and determine the three types of psychological behavior—defensive behavior, maintenance behavior and progressive behavior.

DEFENSIVE BEHAVIOR

Biological homeogretic behavior and psychological defensive behavior defend against death. Biological homeogretic behavior defends against death through processes and sensations such as our immune system, our inflammation system, and movements such as our fight or flight instincts.

Sexual defensive behavior defends against rejection through pornography, masturbation, and fantasy. Physical defensive behavior defends against death through physical structures such as doctors, hospitals, police, and armies. Mental defensive behavior defends against death through mental behavior such as humor, understanding, values, opinions, and beliefs.[7] We defend against death before we devote energy to maintaining or prolonging life.

Our unique defensive physical behavior that defends against physical illness, injury and pain is the basis for unique defensive mental behavior that defends against mental illness, injury, and pain. Just as we instinctively avoid negative physical reinforcement so too do we avoid negative mental reinforcement. We learn that "Not having what you want is wanting what you have." (i.e. "Learning to want" what you have).[8] We focus on the good things that we have. Again in the words of a popular song:

> *When I am worried and cannot sleep, I count my blessings instead of sheep,*
> *And I fall asleep counting my blessings*
> *When my bankroll is getting small, I think of when I had none at all.*
> *And I fall asleep counting my blessings.[9]*

The result of these defense mechanisms is that we automatically focus on and devote our energy to the type of behavior that is successful. Similarly, we try to avoid, and if necessary discount the importance of, the

---

7. There are also many types of ignorant or sick defensive behavior such as psychotic, immature or neurotic defensive behavior but we are only talking here about "knowledgeable" defensive behavior. In other words, knowledgeable defensive behavior is behavior that successfully contributes to an individual's survival in a collective environment even if it temporarily limits development. Like a fever or a limp, defensive behavior limits our functioning but helps us get through a rough period.

8. Cheryl Trigg. "I'm Going to Soak Up the Sun."

9.Irving Berlin. "Count Your Blessings Instead of Sheep."

types of behavior in which we are least successful. When we are unable to avoid negative reinforcement, we adjust our values, opinions, and beliefs to discount the importance of that negative reinforcement. *In very simple terms,* the poor need more economic defenses to justify why they are not rich, and the wealthy need more political defenses to justify why they are not more generous.

MAINTENANCE BEHAVIOR

Biological homeostatic behavior and psychological maintenance behavior maintain equilibriums. Biological homeostatic behavior maintains equilibriums through physical constants that maintain the correct amount of glucose and sucrose in our blood, our blood temperature at 98.6 degrees etc. Sexual maintenance behavior maintains homeostatic equilibriums of estrogen and testosterone through sex and nurturing. Physical maintenance behavior maintain homeostatic equilibriums through physical habits such as eating, drinking, working, and physical structures such as furnaces, air conditioners, refrigerators and plumbing. Mental maintenance behavior maintains mental homeostatic equilibriums through tolerance, a balance between work and play, relaxation and stress, positive reinforcement, and negative reinforcement. We maintain equilibriums before we prolong life. The advantages of mutually beneficial behaviors teach us to adjust to different units of survival by changing our roles when we are with our family or friends, at work or in a foreign country.

Just as our homeostatic processes take up most of our biological energy, so too do our maintenance processes take up most of our psychological energy.

PROGRESSIVE BEHAVIOR

Biological homeorhetic behavior and psychological progressive behavior prolongs life. Biological homeorhetic behavior prolongs life through intercourse, growth, and reproduction. Sexual progressive behavior prolongs life through touching, talking, kissing, intercourse, and family. Physical progressive behavior prolongs life through conditioning and practice, as well as familial, organizational, and national structures. Mental progressive behavior prolongs life through mental behavior such as study, thinking, creating, introspection, and reflection.

Defensive and maintenance behavior help supply basic drives and needs and thus make life easier and more comfortable. Progressive behavior, however, involves learning and understanding and increases our historical survival through our ability to contribute to others. These behaviors contribute to others directly as well as indirectly through impersonal cultural structures such as artifacts, infrastructure, norms, morals, laws, etc.

The challenge for any individual, family, or nation is to maximize the energy devoted to progressive behavior and minimize the energy devoted to defensive and maintenance behavior. Biologically, we prioritize our energy toward homeogretic needs (recovering from illness, injury and attaining safety) and homeostatic needs (food, water and sleep) before we can attend to homeorhetic needs (growth and reproduction). Similarly, psychologically, we prioritize our energy toward defensive needs (avoiding negative reinforcement) and maintenance needs (protecting our family or making money) before we devote our energy to progressive needs (learning, understanding and contributing to others).

However, biological behavior is never static. We utilize food, warmth, sex, and safety to obtain homeostasis. The moment we achieve equilibrium the situation changes--we grow (i.e. we achieve the progressive equilibrium of homeorhesis), or we receive an injury or grow older (i.e. we endure the regressive equilibrium of homeogresis).

Similarly, psychological behavior is never static. When we have satisfied our mental needs for information (mental food), love (mental warmth), and safety (mental money), we achieve a mental equilibrium of happiness. However, the moment that state is achieved a progressive or regressive state follows. With information, training, love, and money, we develop, learn, and adjust to a progressive equilibrium, after a temporary state of contentment. Conversely, with ignorance, sickness, pain, failure and the loss of money, companionship, and confidence, we adjust to a regressive equilibrium, after a temporary state of discontentment. Therefore, our situation is never static. We are never "happy" just the way we are. We can only achieve happiness through constantly learning and loving just as we can only achieve biological fulfillment through constantly growing and reproducing.[10]

Our unconscious biological behavior is the basis for our conscious psychological behavior. Just as our automatic biological behavior compares constants with unconscious and subconscious stimulation and reacts and responds to maintain equilibriums, so too do we use our conscious psychological processes to compare our physical environment, feelings, and reasoning to determine the behavior that will maintain equilibrium. In each case, we adjust for whether we can quickly correct the drives and, needs and or whether they require longer-term adjustments. Homeostatic adjustments are correctable immediately such as drinking water to reduce thirst. In contrast, homeogretic and homeorhetic adjustments take longer and result in longer-term changes

---

10, When we are older, learning replaces growth and pleasurable intercourse replaces reproductive intercourse.

such as injury, illness, or growth. Similarly, psychological maintenance adjustments are correctable immediately. In contrast, psychological defensive and progressive adjustments take longer. Just as we avoid exposure to physical cold through houses and clothes, we avoid mental cold through relationships and norms and impersonal mental cold through tolerance and freedom. Our genes store the ideal biological constants and central nervous system comparators. These biological constants provide an example of ideal psychological constants. We extrapolate from biological constants to psychological constants. The psychological constant of beauty comes from historical behavior and traditional, political, and artistic feelings that make us *feel we want to survive*. The psychological constant of truth comes from historical behavior and social, economic, and scientific reasoning that enables us to *understand how to survive*. These psychological constants and comparators are mental operating systems that help us select capable behavior that we feel and think is most likely to correct disequilibrium, defend against death, or maintain and improve our chances for survival. This capable behavior includes working to make money, playing to feel like living, and learning to obtain a more passionate, meaningful and purposeful life.

CAPABLE BEHAVIOR

"Out, out, brief candle! Life's but a walking shadow, a poor player that struts and frets his hour upon the stage, and then is heard no more; it is a tale told by an idiot, full of sound and fury signifying nothing." [11]

—*Macbeth*

While there are tremendous benefits from living in a collective

---

11. Macbeth Act five, Scene 5. William Shakespeare

environment, the greatest challenge for each of us is to maintain a healthy sense of self-worth while living closely in environments with others who are brighter, handsomer, healthier, stronger, wealthier, more powerful, and more famous than we are. In order to survive, we must be informed of that reality but not feel threatened by it. We gain that capacity through 'triangularization.' We gain that capacity through:

- Knowing what our role is and what the role is for others through logical self-knowledge;
- Feeling that our role is worthwhile though emotional self-knowledge and,
- Integrating own unique emotional and logical self-knowledge into behavior that maximizes our survival.

Self-knowledge allows us to do this by developing feelings and reasoning that suit our own unique behavior within our environment. Although Shakespeare's Macbeth states "We are but poor players who strut and fret our hour upon the stage and are heard from no more" we are, in fact, incredible actors. We learn new lines (learn new emotional and logical behavior) every day as the play (our environment and our position in our environment) changes. We also constantly learn to play different roles by integrating our emotional and logical behavior. Therefore, all choices require internal self-knowledge about how one can best be able to use one's capabilities to cooperate with others emotionally. Similarly, all choices require external self-knowledge about how one can best be able to use one's capabilities to cooperate logically. This dual approach to cooperation makes human choices complex. One can cooperate by nurturing, teaching, supporting, consoling, and inspiring others through art and beauty. Similarly, one can cooperate by competing, being competent and protecting, providing, and motivating others through science and truth. Ignorance is being skilled in feelings *or* reasoning without appreciating both feelings *and* reasoning. Intelligence is admiring and respecting *both* feelings *and* reasoning. Moreover, we apply these behaviors to our different roles as child, spouse, parent, employee, citizen etc. More incredible yet, we learn to feel that each role we play is meaningful and purposeful.

We are able to develop our feelings about these changing roles through emotional behavior. Just as we focus our eyes biologically on meaningful information (movement) that enables us to survive, so too do we focus our feelings on meaningful information (our successes) to make us feel like we want to survive. This emotional selection process maximizes our sense of self-worth, minimizes our sense of worthlessness, and makes us *feel like we want to live* in a collective environment.

Similarly, we are able to develop our reasoning about these changing roles through logical behavior. Just as we focus our eyes biologically on purposeful information that enables us to survive (food), so too do we focus our reasoning *psychologically* on purposeful information (knowledge) that increases our ability to survive. Logical behavior maximizes our ability to survive, avoid death, and *enables us to live* in a collective environment.

5

CONCLUSION

❧

"Now each man judges well the things he knows, and of these he is a good judge. And so the man who has been educated in a subject is a good judge of that subject, and the man who has received an all-round education is a good judge in general. Hence a young man is not a proper hearer of lectures on knowledge: for he is inexperienced in the actions that occur in life, but its discussions start from these and are about these; and further, since he tends to follow his passions, his study will be vain and unprofitable, because the end aimed at is not knowledge but action. And it makes no difference whether he is young in years or youthful in character; the defect does not depend on time, but on his living, and pursuing each successive object, as passion directs. For to such person, as to the incontinent, knowledge brings no profit; but to those who desire and act in accordance with a rational principle, knowledge about such matters will be of great benefit."[12]

---

12. The basic works of Aristotle. ibid. page 935.

The objective of government is to develop our egotistical lower brain consisting of genetic biological knowledge to include a cooperative forebrain consisting of acquired psychological knowledge. The ojective of government is to develop its citizens empathy, reason and competence and by doing so increase a nation's collective survival.

Some of this development process is obvious. However, the stronger the reptilian instincts, the greater the challenge. Our most basic instinct is sex and no where is our passion stronger and our experience and reason less than in our teenage years. Religions, norms, customs, and traditions place their strongest commandments on marriage and reproduction. However, if we are ever to be successful in avoiding a future Armageddon, our biological instinct for egotistical sex must be developed into a pschologoical capability for responsible reproduction.

If we look at our other instincts we can see we are far more objective about their development. For example, we have developed sight through glasses, binoculars, telescopes, magnifying glasses, and microsopes. We have developed movement through horses, cars, trains, ariplanes, and rockets. And no one, except perhaps the Amish, objects to using this knowledge. In contrast, our development of the sexual instinct is much more restrictive. Many religions still have restrictions on family planning and women's education. What we need to do is elaborate the difference between sexual pleasure and responsible reproduction. To do so we must substantially increase our sexual knowledge about the objective for having children.

Sexual knowledge has to do with our feelings that we want to reproduce and our capacity to be able to reproduce. Sexual knowledge is dependent upon the development of our sexual instincts. Biologicallly, what enables us to survive is physical health. Psychologically what enables us able to survive is mental health. Biologically, what makes us able to survive after death sexually is to have healthy children. Psychologically, what makes us able to survive after death sexually is to have children who have the resources, reinforcement, and training to develop a meaningful and purposeful life.

Unfortunately, most of our efforts on sexual development focus on biological sex and physical survival rather than psychological meaning, parenting and mental survival. They focus on efforts to resolve the problem of the disadvantaged through "Head Start" programs and racial preferences. This approach is like trying to resolve the problem of polio by treating polio victims rather than developing a polio vaccine. The problem of disadvantaged children needs to be addressed before pregnancy, not after birth.

Most people believe a discussion of responsible parenting is a racial issue. Nothing could be further from the truth. Responsible parenting in the U.S. is a cultural issue that applies to nearly half our population, not just to minorities.

According to the Guttmacher Institute, half of all pregnancies in the U.S. are unintended. Similarly, according to the U. S. Census Bureau, in 2013 35% of all children lived in single parent households. Finally, according to the U. S. Center for Disease Control and Prevention, only 56% of children born from 2011-2013 were born to married parents. Fully 44% were born to unmarried parents.[13] This number of unmarried parents has increased from 36% in 2002. While we must get a license to fish or hunt and even pass a test to obrain a drivers license, we have no requirements at all for having a child. We provide free medical assistance and make it difficult for pregnant mothers of unwanted children to have

13. Twenty six percent were born to cohabiting but unmarried parents and 18% were born to single parents.

an abortlion. We even allow women on heroin to give birth to heroin addicted babies – certainly as clear an example of a crime against humanity as anything in Nazi Germany.

As in the case of cigarette smoking, we have the capability to reinforce and train better family choices and more responsible parenting. We have the capacity to require insurance companies to pay for contraceptions and abortions and to ensure our schools provide training in family planing. We have the capacity to require both parents (or a second responsible adult) be committed to providing for and being responsible for each child until adulthood. We have the capacity to require both parents not be on welfare or drugs when having a baby. We have the capacity to require both parents who want a child to be trained in childcare. We have the capacity to demonstrate the cost to society of raising and educating a child which the parents cannot afford to raise and educate. And we have the capacity to demonstrate the detrimental affects of a 33% increase in the population on our climate, government and economy.

Why then do such common sense proposals seem so politically naïve? Why do these changes seem impossible in a democratic society? The answer would appear to be due to insufficient sexual knowledge.

Because childbirth is such a basic instinct, attitudes and norms about having children are deeply entrenched in religions and traditions. On the other hand, religions and traditions are the most basic part of our defensive knowledge that maintains our desire to live. Furthermore, religions and traditions are critical to the survival of any modern democratic nation. If people believe doing unto others as you would have them do unto you gets you into heaven, what sensible government would try to discourage this admonition. In a democracy, whatever people believe about life after death, as long as it does not harm others, is a source of strength. On the other hand, due to a lack of knowledge, religions and traditions also transmit dysfunctional defensive knowledge about family planning. How then do we change those aspects of religions and traditions that are dysfunctional to collective survival without lessening the importance of religions and traditions?

The answer would appear to be in the same manner that we changed attitudes towards cigarette smoking. Just as we made aggressive attacks on the dishonesty of cigarette companies, we can attack the dishonesty of those who discourage family planning. Just as we provided positive reinforcement for those who stopped smoking and negative reinforcement for those who continue to smoke, we can provide positive reinforcement for family planning and negative reinforcement for unplanned families. Just as we provide education and warnings for smokers, we can provide education and warnings for prospective parents. They key point is that all of these changes can occur within our democratic and capitalistic framework and within the concept of free choice. Positive and negative reinforcement do not prevent people from smoking but merely encourage and discourage them from making an unhealthy choice. Similarly, positive and negative reinforcement will not eliminate under nourished, under nurtured, under structured and unloved children from being born but will merely discourage potential parents from making unplanned and underprovided for family choices.

Our Declaration of Independence states that we are endowed with certain inalienable rights. Certainly, one of those rights must the right to have sex with any other consenting adult. On the other hand, while having sex is a personal choice, having a baby is a social choice as well.

71

The responsibility of having a child is the most important responsibility an adult will ever undertake. The responsibility of raising healthy and educated citizens is also the most important responsibility that a government will ever undertake. Therefore, should not having a child have the same government requirement about being educated about family planning as we do about being educated in general? If we are to avoid an Armageddon, we must be willing to devote as many resources to developing this sexual knowledge as we do to developing physical and mental knowledge.

The question is how to provide the resources for the research necessary to demonstrate the enormous cost of unplanned parenting in a democratic society. The answer would appear to be though contributions from the wealthy through their foundations. The costs of unplanned, under nurtured and underprovided for children we know is enormous. The U. S. Department of Agriculture estimates the average cost of raising a child born in 2013 until age 18, for a middle income family in the U. S., is approximately $245,000. If the child's parents do not pay for these costs through their taxes, other citizens must make up the shortfall through increases in their own taxes to pay for the child's education, health care and welfare. Everyone knows that children raised in affluent households do substantially better than those raised in impoverished households. Everyone knows that children raised in a household with mature parents with two or three children do substantially better than children raised in a household with teenage parents. with five or six children.

As discussed earlier, the primary source of sexual knowledge is family nourishment, nurturing, passion, and love. Unfortunately, society, in spite of the best of intentions, cannot put in what parents have left out.

Therefore, what society must do is try to reduce irresponsible parenting. What is missing, however, is the research that demonstrates how enormous the costs of irresponsible parenting is to society. Just as we had to clarify, beyond a reasonable doubt, the health statistics on cigarette smoking, so, too, do we have to clarify beyond a reasonable doubt the costs to society of irresponsible parenting.

In the case of cigarette smoking, once we had clarified the relationship between cigarettes and cancer, we attacked and sued the disseminators of false and dysfunctional information about cigarette smoking. For cigarettes, this meant the cigarette companies. For irresponsible parenting, this means anti-abortion and anti-family planning advocates. For cigarettes, we restricted the right to purchase cigarettes for minors through legislation.

- If we can demonstrate beyond a reasonable doubt that planned children are substantially better citizens[14] than unplanned children, would the world really be so bad if unmarried prospective parents had to register before having children? We already require that we have to register before we can vote.

- If we can demonstrate beyond a reasonable doubt that children of mature parents are substantially better citizens than children of teenage parents are, would the world really be so bad if prospective parents were encouraged to be at least eigthteen years old? We already require children be eighteen before they can buy cigarettes and drive a car.

- If we can demonstrate beyond a reasonable doubt that children of parents who graduated from junior high school are substantially better citizens than children of parents who did not graduate from junior high school, would the world really be so bad if prospective

---

14. Better citizens means bettter educated and higher income citizens.

parents were encouraged to graduate from junior high school or pass a test on parenting before they had a child? We already require future drivers to pass a written driving test before they can obtain a driver's license.

- If we can demonstrate beyond a reasonable doubt that children of non-drug using parents are substantially better citizens than children of drug using parents, would the world really be so bad if prospective parents had to demonstrate that they were not on drugs? We already require that drivers not drive under the influence of alcohol.

- If we can demonstrate beyond a reasonable doubt that children of non-welfare parents are substantially better citizens than children of welfare parents, would the world really be so bad if prospective parents were encouraged not to have children while on welfare? We already require that drivers have the resources to buy insurance and have an insurance company willing to insure them before they can drive.

- If we can demonstrate beyond a reasonable doubt that children of two parents are substantially better citizens than children of single parents, would the world really be so bad if both parents were encouraged to accept financial and parental responsibility for a child? We already have divorce laws that require both parents be responsible financially for children in a divorce.

We could easily pass and implement these laws and requirements, if we sufficiently clarified for the electorate the current costs of not implementing such changes. Human selection selects behavior that leads to progress. More wanted, loved, and educated babies are more important to progress than cleaner environments and more prosperity. Not recognizing and responding to this fact will lead to wars, depressions, plagues and an Armageddon. 74

DEFENSIVE KNOWLEDGE THAT AVOIDS DEATH

DEFENSIVE SURVIVAL FORCES	That Reinforce Defensive Feelings To Avoid	And Train Defensive Reasoning To Avoid	That Leads to Defensive Capacities	That Develop Defensive Capabilities	That Avoids Feelings of Unhappiness Through	That results in DEFENSIVE BEHAVIOR
TYPES OF GENETIC PERSONAL SEXUAL, PHYSICAL AND MENTAL DEFENSIVE CAPABILITIES						
Sexual Drives	Loneliness	Rejection	Defensive Hardware	Personal Defensive Responses	Sexual *Masturbation*	Personal Coordinated Sexual Behavior
Physical Drives	Hunger	Defeat	Defensive Firmware	Personal Defensive Habits	Bodily *Comfort*	Personal Coordinated Physical Behavior
Mental Drives	Fear	Indifference	Defensive Applications	Personal Defensive Skills	Mental *Egotism*	Personal Coordinated Mental Behavior

THAT RESULT IN COLLECTIVE INTERPERSONAL FAMILY, NATIONAL and CONCEPTUAL DEFENSIVE CAPABILITIES						
Family Drives	Divorce	Fighting	Defensive Platforms	Interpersonal Defensive Values	Family *Indifference*	Interpersonal Coordinated Family Behavior
National Drives	Unemployment	Demonstrating	Defensive Software	Interpersonal Defensive Abilities	National *Greed*	Interpersonal Coordinated National Behavior
Conceptual Drives	Meaninglessness	Purposelessness	Defensive Operating Systems	Interpersonal Defensive Principles	Conceptual *Defensiveness*	Interpersonal Coordinated Conceptual Behavior

THAT RESULT IN CULTURAL IMPERSONAL FAMILY, NATIONAL and CONCEPTUAL DEFENSIVE CAPABILITIES						
Family Needs	Prejudiced Environments	Rigid Environments	Defensive Family Environments	Defensive Imp. Values	Family *Conflict*	Impersonal Coordinated Family Behavior
National Needs	Discriminatory Environments	Hostile Environments	Defensive National Envir.	Defensive Imp Abilities	National *Complaining*	Impersonal Coordinated National Behavior
Conceptual Needs	Apathetic Environments	Dysfunctional Environments	Defensive Conceptual Environments	Defensive Impersonal Principles	Conceptual *Self-Righteousness*	Impersonal Coordinated Conceptual Behavior

MAINTENANCE KNOWLEDGE THAT MAINTAINS LIFE

MAINTENANCE SURVIVAL FORCS	That Reinforce Maintenance Feelings Through	And Train Maintenance Reasoning Through	That Leads to Maintenance Capacities	That Develop Maintenance Capabilities	That Result in Feelings of Equilibrium Through	That Results in MAINTENANCE BEHAVIOR
TYPES OF GENETIC PERSONAL SEXUAL, PHYSICAL AND MENTAL MAINTENANCE CAPABILITIES						
Sexual Drives	Sensual Sensations	Motor Movements	Maintenance Hardware	Maintenance Responses	Sexual Equilibrium	Personal Cooperative Sexual Behavior
Physical Drives	Physical Nurturing	Physical Competitiveness	Maintenance Firmware	Maintenance Habits	Physical Equilibrium	Personal Cooperative Bodily Behavior
Mental Drives	Mental Values	Mental Routines	Maintenance Applications	Maintenance Skills	Mental Equilibrium	Personal Cooperative Mental Behavior
THAT RESULT IN COLLECTIVE INTERPERSONAL FAMILY, NATIONAL and CONCEPTUAL MAINTENANCE CAPABILITIES						
Family Drives	Social Relationships	Traditional Norms	Maintenance Platforms	Maintenance Values	Family Equilibrium	Interpersonal Cooperative Family Behavior
National Drives	Economic Work	Political Opinions	Maintenance Software	Maintenance Abilities	National Equilibrium	Interpersonal Cooperative National Behavior
Conceptual Drives	Aesthetic Insights	Scientific Reflections	Maintenance Operating Systems	Maintenance Principles	Conceptual Equilibrium	Interpersonal Cooperative Cognitive Behavior
THAT RESULT IN CULTURAL IMPERSONAL FAMILY, NATIONAL and CONCEPTUAL MAINTENANCE CAPABILITIES						
Family Needs	Social Environments	Traditional Environments	Maintenance Family Environments	Maintenance Impersonal Values	Family Equilibrium	Impersonal Cooperative Family Behavior
National Needs	Economic Environments	Political Environments	Maintenance National Environments	Maintenance Impersonal Abilities	National Equilibrium	Impersonal Cooperative National Behavior
Conceptual Needs	Aesthetic Environments	Scientific Environments	Maintenance Conceptual Environments	Maintenance Impersonal Principles	Conceptual Equilibrium	Impersonal Cooperative Conceptual Behavior

PROGRESSIVE KNOWLEDGE THAT PROLONGS LIFE

POSITIVE SURVIVAL FORCES	That Reinforce Progressive Feelings From	And Train Purposeful Autonomous* Reasoning From	That Leads to Progressive Capacities	That Develop Progressive Capabilities	That Result in Feelings of Happiness Through	That results in PROGRESSIVE BEHAVIOR
		TYPES OF GENETIC PERSONAL SEXUAL, PHYSICAL AND MENTAL PROGRESSIVE CAPABILITIES				
Sexual Drives	Sensual Sensations	Motor Movement	Progressive Hardware	Progressive Personal Responses	Sexual Pleasure	Personal Contributive Sexual Behavior
Physical Drives	Kind Nurturing	Fair Competitiveness	Progressive Firmware	Progressive Personal Habits	Bodily Health	Personal Contributive Physical Behavior
Mental Drives	Empathetic Caring	Honest Objectivity	Progressive Applications	Progressive Personal Skills	Personal Satisfaction	Personal Contributive Mental Behavior
		THAT RESULT IN COLLECTIVE INTERPERSONAL, FAMILY, NATIONAL and CONCEPTUAL PROGRESSIVE CAPABILITIES				
Family Drives	Loving Relationships	Moral Norms	Progressive Platforms	Progressive Interpersonal Values	Interpersonal Commitment	Interpersonal Contributive Family Behavior
National Drives	Competent Work	Ethical Cooperation	Progressive Software	Progressive Interpersonal Abilities	Interpersonal Success	Interpersonal Contributive National Behavior
Conceptual Drives	Beautiful Meaningful-ness	Truthful Purposeful-ness	Progressive Operating Systems	Progressive Interpersonal Principles	Interpersonal Satisfaction	Interpersonal Contributive Conceptual Behavior
		THAT RESULT IN CULTURAL IMPERSONAL, FAMILY, NATIONAL and CONCEPTUAL PROGRESSIVE CAPABILITIES				
Family Needs	Loyal Environments	Moral Environ,	Progressive Family Environments	Progressive Imp. Values	Impersonal Joy	Impersonal Contributive Family Behavior
National Needs	Competent Environments	Ethical Environ	Progressive National Environments	Progressive Impersonal Abilities	Impersonal Happiness	Impersonal Contributive National Behavior
Conceptual Needs	Beautiful Environments	Truthful Environ	Progressive Conceptual Environments	Progressive Impersonal Principles	Cognitive Contentment	Impersonal Contributive Conceptual Behavior

www.ingramcontent.com/pod-product-compliance
Lightning Source LLC
La Vergne TN
LVHW091208080426
835509LV00006B/894